Christmas Jesus

Seven Gifts God Gives Us

Dave Holland

Copyright Information

Christmas Jesus

ASIN: B081ZHCJM9; **ISBN:** 9781517287245

Table of Contents

*Loving God, help us remember the
birth of Jesus,
that we may share in the
song of the angels,
the gladness of the shepherds,
and the worship of the wise men.*

Robert Louis Stevenson

Introduction

The Son of God did not erupt on the scene. Instead, He slipped through the sheets of time to join us on our dark planet.

I mean this small book to be an appetizer, a foretaste of things to come. It is an inexpensive preview of my daily devotionals, *Every Day Jesus and Extraordinary Jesus*. This work is also a road map to Christmas joy. Read it to discover how to plot your course by bringing Jesus into focus this holiday season.

To retail businesses, Christmas is the greatest profit-making machine in the history of humanity. Advertisements incessantly prod us to buy more gifts. But what is Christmas really about? At its core is a baby who simply wants to give you gifts—especially Himself. Besides His Son, God gives us seven wonderful gifts to help us find our footing on the path to the heart of Jesus. This book presents you with those seven bountiful treasures.

In this new, revamped edition of Christmas Jesus I have added three fiction fables. These are my offering to you for your enjoyment and edification. I had children in mind when I wrote Fable 3, "When God Called Saint Nick," but I also hope it will speak to your inner child. We live in times when we could use more fun and a sense of wonder in our lives.

Christmas Jesus is primarily a gathering of devotions solely drawn from the Gospel of Luke. This gospel targets us in the Western world. Doctor Luke is the only Gentile to write a book of the Bible. He is an educated doctor and historian. He conveys the life of Christ to us by his zealous faith, partnered with sound research. For instance, he probably interviewed Mary extensively to give us an accurate and intimate rendering of the birth of the Messiah.

This book is an introduction to the larger devotional Bible study called *Every Day Jesus,* a forty-day devotional that covers the first five chapters of Luke. It includes the words of Luke paragraph by paragraph with some explanation, application, and prayer. The goal is to follow Jesus day by day, event by event, until His path becomes our path. I'm sure you'll enjoy the journey.

I discovered something remarkable during my ten years of study in the Gospel of Luke. The text is without doctrinal or theological bias. Those words encourage Protestants, Catholics, Evangelicals and Charismatics, alike. The narrative even speaks to observers who simply want to know more about the history-altering figure named Jesus.

We can unite around that beautiful Savior. My goal here is to present Jesus in all His unadorned and untheological glory. Please join me in saying, *Happy Birthday Jesus!*

God Gives Us Humility

LIQUID FIRE

For my eyes have seen your salvation, which you have prepared in the sight of all people, a light for revelation to the Gentiles and for glory to your people Israel. Luke 2:30-32

Gently falling snow paved my walk to our village church on Christmas Eve so long ago. We lived a few blocks from the church I pastored in that small New England town, and I expected the Light of the World to visit us as we celebrated His birth. I was preparing early for a full house of festive worshippers on my first Christmas Eve Service. Life could not have been better—until it wasn't.

I approached our small white colonial church building with the tall steeple noting it looked so warm and inviting. The church and the stained-glass windows glowed with subtle glory, waiting for the people to arrive.

The first to come was the woman with Christ's birthday cake, baked in the shape of a cross. Someone came up with the idea that since it was Jesus' birthday, *He* should have a cake. I expounded on the idea by saying, "Hey, why don't we conclude the service with everyone lighting their candles as we sing 'Silent Night' and process to the front of the church putting our candles in the cake?" That's when peace on earth almost became hell in church.

Nearly two hundred souls crowded into the church the night of our dear Savior's birth, far exceeding my expectations. Children fidgeted during scripture readings. People sang Christmas carols with gusto while angels sang harmony. Ushers efficiently distributed the communion elements, and everyone solemnly partook of the body and blood of the Lord Jesus. I mused it was the perfect Christmas Eve service. The time had come for the grand finale.

I directed people toward the four-foot-long birthday cake baked for sweet baby Jesus and gave the fateful instructions, "Ushers, turn out the lights and ignite the candle of the person on the end of each row, then each one lite your neighbor's candles for the glory of God as we all sing, 'Silent Night' processing by the cake." The radiant glow of the room grew with increasing intensity as people came forward to place their candle in the now shining cake. As two hundred wax candles accumulated, the cake transformed from beaming to a blazing inferno. The strangest sight unfolded in slow motion. Liquid fire flowed over the edges of the cake onto the floor and the young pastor thought, "Oh my Lord, I'm going to burn down the church with all the people in it!"

Miraculously, the fire went out as soon as the flames hit the floor. No one fried that night. "Praise God in the Highest," the angels surely sang. A little boy in the back who didn't get to place his candle in the cake began crying, "But Daddy, I want to start a fire too."

The lights quickly came back on and the parishioners went home that night, glad to be alive. One look from my wife silently said, "You silly, silly man."

I'm thankful the grace of God did not allow us to burn that night. This event reminds me that Jesus came to save sinners of whom I am chief. I learned Christmas is not about lights or candles, cakes or carols, but entirely about a Savior who loves us enough to become one of us. I went home a humbler man that Christmas Eve as I realized God was preparing *me* for the birth of His Son in my heart. The first quality we need to welcome Jesus this Christmas is the humility to know that life is really all about Jesus, the King of Kings.

Lord Jesus, help us focus on You during our Christmas celebrations. Too often we obsessed over decorations and liturgies rather than on the Son of God/. We want to see You, Jesus, touch You, worship You in all Your glory. You are the present that we seek. You are the Light of our lives.

God Gives Us Ears to Hear

ANSWER THE PHONE

> *But the angel said to him: "Do not be afraid,*
> *Zechariah; your prayer has been heard. Your wife Elizabeth*
> *will bear you a son, and you are to give him the name John.*
> *He will be a joy and delight to you, and many will rejoice*
> *because of his birth, for he will be great in the sight of the*
> *Lord. He is never to take wine or other fermented drink,*
> *and he will be filled with the Holy Spirit even from birth.*
> *Many of the people of Israel will he bring back to the Lord*
> *their God. And he will go on before the Lord, in the spirit*
> *and power of Elijah, to turn the hearts of the fathers to their*
> *children and the disobedient to the wisdom of the righteous-to*
> *make ready a people prepared for the Lord."* Luke 1:13-17

God is preparing us for something more. He is patiently formulating His plans with great forethought. We will find fulfillment only when we discover God's purpose for our lives. God is calling, but will we answer the phone? Are we open to the supernatural move of the Holy Spirit breaking into our lives? Listen to the voice calling you from the wilderness, "Prepare the way of the Lord."

John the Baptist had the luxury of knowing why he was born, and Luke 1:13-17 reveals that purpose - to lead others to faith in the Messiah. The people had not heard from God in over four hundred years. They needed a *now* word from God plowing their hearts open to receive the seed of life found in Christ. God's intention for John required purity of life, fullness of the Holy Spirit, and power to invite people back to the Lord.

John didn't perform wonders or miracles. He never raised the dead or healed the sick, yet Jesus said that no one was greater. John prepared the way for Christ by crying out to God's people, *REPENT!* In essence, he preached, "turn away from the mundane things that distract you and devote yourself to God." Those words are just as valid today.

"Repent!" is too often the word we do not want to hear. Allow me to share what repentance is not—mourning over your past misdeeds and shameful behaviors. God does not want you to crawl to Him like a worm or grovel as a poor, shameless creature.

Repentance means to change the way you think. Allow God to affect your mind and redirect your heart toward Him. Jesus came to facilitate that process. Place your trust in Christ and He removes the guilt. Then, live joyfully with the approval that God gives you through His Son—He's yours now through repentance and faith!

Think of repentance this way - God is on the telephone calling you, and John, the prophet in our passage, pleads, "pick up the phone and listen to the Lord!" God desires a conversation that brings us closer to Him. The result of that turning away becomes real and visible as we reconcile with our Creator and return to His ways.

Good gardeners know that to produce a harvest, you must first prepare the earth, break open the fallow ground, fertilize the soil and sow good seed. No preparation, no sowing, no harvest. The same is true for us. Good things happen when we turn toward the Lord and invite God to roto till our hearts and sow fresh grace. The Holy Spirit will saturate your soul like spring rain.

Allow God to speak into your life through the voice of His Word. Let the Holy Spirit direct your attention back to Him. Is there anything more important than that?

I think not.

I remember Jack Hayford singing, *Let us search and try our ways and turn again to the Lord, lift our hearts with our hands unto God in the heavens and return again to the Lord.* [1] That song demonstrates the spirit of repentance.

When I became a Christian at sixteen years of age, I thought I was the first confessing Christian in our family. I discovered the back-story while I was in Bible College. During my mother's pregnancy with me, she had been an active Christian. A great gulf of antagonism separated my mom and dad. The doctor told my mother that if she didn't improve her emotional state, she would lose her baby. My mother desperately called upon the Lord praying, *Lord, if you spare this child, I will dedicate him to You and name him David.*

Later, my parents divorced. In the years following their breakup, my mother slowly drifted away from God. Despite her shortcomings, the Lord was faithful in answering her prayer. He claimed me for Himself.

I answered God's call because of the prayer that went before me. John the Baptist followed the prophetic call because of the prayer and events that occurred before he was even born. God is reaching out to you through the events of your life as well. God wove His grace into the fabric of your history. Ask God to give you the eyes to see His mercy working in your life.

The Lord yearns for us not only to respond to His invitation, but also to pray for others, drawing them to the kingdom of God. Christ Jesus the Lord is calling your name right now!

Will you pick up the phone and answer Him?

Will you also pray for others to answer His call?

The joy of life resides in living beyond ourselves and dedicating our lives to God's purpose. The second quality needed to receive the newborn King this Christmas is having an ear that will listen and return to God.

---

[1] Hayford, Jack M. *Sing Praises, A Collection of Songs and Hymns for Today's Church on the Way.* Van Nuys, California, 1976: page 36.

My King and My God, open my ears to hear You as I turn toward You today. Make Your plans and purposes known to me as You did to the prophet, John the Baptist. I want to serve You as faithfully as He did. Prepare my heart to receive Jesus the Christ, the Son of the Living God. I ask that I could also be Your Voice speaking Your Word in the wilderness of this world. Examine my heart, purify my motives, and sharpen my focus I pray. I must be an open ear listening to Your Voice—help me hear Your call and answer the phone. In Jesus' Name, I pray, amen.

God Gives Us His Spirit

THE SPIRIT-FORMED LIFE

"How will this be," Mary asked the angel, "since I am a virgin?"

The angel answered, "The Holy Spirit will come upon you, and the power of the Most High will overshadow you. So the holy one to be born will be called the Son of God. Even Elizabeth your relative is going to have a child in her old age, and she who was said to be barren is in her sixth month. For nothing is impossible with God."

"I am the Lord's servant," Mary answered. "May it be to me as you have said." Then the angel left her.
Luke 1:34-38

My child-like interpretation of Luke 1:31 goes something like, *Surprise! Mary, there's a baby in your belly conceived by the Holy Spirit.* This simple promise to Mary holds tremendous provision for us. The birth of Christ is beyond eloquent words, so the Angel of the Lord just says it like it is - the Holy Spirit is forming the Son of God in you. Jesus is the ultimate Spirit-formed life.

Mary's conception of the Savior was unique to the human experience as the Holy Spirit overshadowed her. God's explanation of the whole matter to Joseph in Matthew 1:20 pronounces *that which is conceived in her is of the Holy Spirit.* In my words, the Holy Spirit breathed on Mary, imparting to her the genesis of spiritual life. His Life–a God quality of Life–that He passed on to us.

The psalmist of Israel, King David, drew on prophetic insight when he penned, *For You formed my inward parts; You covered me in my mother's womb. I will praise You, for I am fearfully and wonderfully made* (Psalm 139:13-14, NKJV). David knew it was God at work in his mother's womb, knitting the strands of his life together. God formed David in His own image. God involves Himself directly in David's formation, and He takes part in our development as well.

Our problem is that sin pollutes us right down to our DNA. Our faults and failures wound us and leave us lying face down in a spiritual ditch. We inherited a stained bloodline from Adam and Eve. Unseemly passions compounded by the influence of a corrupt culture moved by unrestrained earthly drives leave us in a raunchy pit.

We fill our lives with lust for more money, more power, more sex. Well, more of anything that makes us feel good.

Paul speaks to our dilemma. *I beseech you therefore, brethren, by the mercies of God, that you present your bodies a living sacrifice, holy, acceptable to God, which is your reasonable service. And do not be conformed to this world, but be transformed by the renewing of your mind, that you may prove what is that good and acceptable and perfect will of God.* Romans 12:1-2, NKJV. Don't allow the corrupting elements of the world into your mind and life.

The same God-power that formed Christ in Mary's womb now desires to shape you and me through the experiences of our lives. Difficulties intended to move us toward the Lord's work like a carpenter's sandpaper to smooth our rough edges. Victories point us Godward in praise—every time we turn to worship—we are further shaped into Christ's likeness.

The scars of divorce and false accusations marred the middle years of my life. I lived emotionally devastated and financially wrecked. As I sat in front of my computer preparing to submit job applications, I thought, *I'm not married now. I'm not in the ministry, I can go anywhere I want on this computer.* Porn, gambling, and raunchy websites abound on the internet. The temptation was intense. But the Holy Spirit spoke quietly to my heart, "What will you become?"

It was a pivotal moment. I could succumb to temptation, or I could yield to the gentle prompting of the Spirit and let Him mold me into a man of God. The Lord focused me on the long-term benefit of following Him, rather than on my short-term desire. God shaped my life through this experience.

The Holy Spirit formed Christ in the womb and Jesus lived a holy life filled with the presence and power of God. He did not succumb to the temptations of the world—He overcame them. His sinless life becomes the key to our freedom from sin. When you put your faith in Jesus, God forms a new creation in you, which was His intention all along.

Through the redemption found in Jesus, we are now free to choose to grow in love, grace, and His Word. Let God's Word and Spirit shape your life into a demonstration of His grace and glory. Allow God's Spirit to form fresh life in you.

Dear God and my Maker, I praise You for the miracle of Christ's incarnation as the God-Man. I thank You He provided the perfect sacrifice for me. Now I pray You would form in me a Christ-likeness. Make me sensitive to Your Spirit as He separates me from the world. Subdue my sin nature and do Your work of re-creation in me. Do this for Your glory, Amen.

God Gives Us Power and Hope

CHARGING BULL

His (John the Baptist) father Zechariah was filled with the Holy Spirit and prophesied:

"Praise be to the Lord, the God of Israel, because he has come and has redeemed his people. He has raised up a horn of salvation for us in the house of his servant David (as he said through his holy prophets of long ago), salvation from our enemies and from the hand of all who hate us - to show mercy to our fathers and to remember his holy covenant, the oath he swore to our father Abraham: to rescue us from the hand of our enemies, and to enable us to serve him without fear in holiness and righteousness before him all our days. And you, my child, will be called a prophet of the Most High; for you will go on before the Lord to prepare the way for him, to give his people the knowledge of salvation through the forgiveness of their sins, because of the tender mercy of our God, by which the rising sun will come to us from heaven to shine on those living in darkness and in the shadow of death, to

19

guide our feet into the path of peace."

And the child grew and became strong in spirit; and he lived in the desert until he appeared publicly to Israel. Luke 1:67-80

The bull paws the ground, gathering his great strength. He snorts hot breath, rhythmically swinging his horns back and forth, slashing the air, preparing to mount a charge of brute force. He is both beautiful and dangerous as he strikes terror into your heart. Such is the power Zechariah attributes to the "horn" of Messiah in Luke 1:67-80.

The priest Zechariah watches the birth of his son, John the Baptist, born to him in old age. God frees his tongue and a melody of thanksgiving arises. In that moment of sheer ecstasy, he utters a song of unparalleled beauty using two Old Testament metaphors that live deep in the marrow of his bones. His son has the mandate to declare the awaited Messiah—the horn of salvation.

The first metaphor refers to the five references in the Psalms that describe the Messiah as *the horn of salvation.* Zechariah picks up the ancient refrain to announce the coming King. The *horn* speaks of Christ's power to protect us from our enemies, to impart mercy from God and to dispel fear. The Creator of the Universe powerfully frees us from the demons of darkness - worry, lust, and anger - to serve God in grace, righteousness, and holiness.

For centuries, people have walked in a misguided fear of God. Guilt, condemnation, and erroneous notions of God render people numb to His grace. *Christ-the-Bull bursts through those barriers,* to lead us to victory over fear, no matter how large or trivial. He fights for us—not against us, mighty to save and deliver!

Zechariah draws from a second metaphor by calling the

Messiah the *Rising Sun* (NIV), or *Dayspring* (NKJV). *The rising sun will come to us from heaven to shine on those living in darkness and the shadow of death, to guide our feet into the path of peace,* Luke 1:78. Luke uses the Greek term *anatello,* translated *rising sun,* meaning *to arise.* Christ is the One through whom light and love come streaming into the world, saying to us, *arise from the darkness of sin, hatred, and selfishness.* The Messiah is the Rising Sun, or Hope-Giver, and His Name is Jesus.

Many people feel like the world conspires against them to inconvenience them. Stressed out Americans, driven to gain the facade of worldly success, are drained of their emotional vitality. Every delay in their day increases their frustration. Rather than living, most people sense they are dying a little more each day. We need the *Rising Sun* to surge upward in our hearts, blazing with the glory of God.

Dayspring Jesus gives us hope that energizes us. Rather than running on empty, Christ fuels us with positive energy, giving us motivation and zest for life. If we dare open our hearts to heaven's hope, it will breed optimistic thoughts and the confidence that God is ordering our steps. Before you die, dear friend, choose to live. Dare to live greatly. Believe and experience God in real-time.

Motivational writer and speaker Ken Blanchard will often begin his speeches with an exercise. He asks the audience to get up and greet those seated around them as if they were insignificant. After many dull, awkward moments, he interrupts them by changing the request. He then asks them to greet people as if they were their long-lost friends or relatives. The energy and vitality in the room immediately elevates. With enthusiasm, people smile, laugh, and hug total strangers.

What changed? Their expectations changed with their hope of a positive response.

Close your eyes and talk to God with new expectations, as though you are talking to the King of Kings, Creator and

Sustainer of the Universe. He has control of your every breath. Zechariah came to see God with the power of a charging bull and the beauty of the rising sun. We should do the same.

The strength of John the Baptist's ministry lies in stirring God's people with an expectation of the Messiah's arrival. *Charging Bull Jesus* wants to burst into our lives, setting us free from the habits and poor choices that have kept us bound.

What burst of new courage does the Lord want to pour into your life today? When we receive that revelation, uncontainable worship will overflow our hearts.

Zechariah received the miracle of a newborn son in his old age and he sang God's praises. God can still do something wonderful in your life if you invite the *Dayspring* Jesus to arise and shine. You were born to reflect the sunlight of Dayspring even as the morning welcomes the light of the sun. Let your praises and good deeds shine.

Dear Lord, You are the horn and power of my salvation—set me free today. You are the Rising Sun of my life - arise in my heart today with healing in Your wings. I sit before You in awe of your great power, but I'm also drawn to Your beautiful majesty. I acknowledge I need You to free me from the thoughts that bring me down—the fear, worry, and anxiety that plagues me. I choose to be confident, whole and well as I put my trust in You. Be strong in my life today, I pray in Jesus' Name. Amen.

Christmas Jesus

*He was created of a mother whom He created.
He was carried by hands that He formed. He
cried in the manger in wordless infancy, He the
Word, without whom all human eloquence is
mute.*

- Augustine

God Gives Us Himself

THE DAY HEAVEN WENT SILENT

*And while they were there, the time came for
her baby to be born. She gave birth to her first child, a
son. She wrapped him snugly in strips of cloth and
laid him in a manger, because there was no room for
them in the village inn.* Luke 2:6

I saw Him, the Ancient of Days, in a vision. I
recognized Him as the Captain of Angel Armies, the Glory of
Heavenly Splendor, the Object of the Father's affections. The
Son was resplendent; He is the Light of very Light, the God of
very God, clothed with power, might and dominion.
Innumerable legions of angelic creatures sang his praises and
marched at His command. Suddenly, without warning, the Son
stood from His throne and strode toward the exit gates of
heaven.

The Son descended from His throne, flinging off his
mantle of omnipotence as the Angel Multitudes gasped. Then
He marched toward the gates discharging His infinite
knowledge. Finally, He drained his omnipresence as He opened
the gates to leave. Jesus abandoned heaven's glory to be born a
vulnerable babe. For the first time in eternity, heaven was

empty of the presence of the Son of God.

"Whoosh! What was that?" the angels cried as the Breath of Heaven blew out the door. He left heaven and poured Himself into a tiny human body far away on the dark planet. Did the music suddenly stop? Were the heavenly hosts perplexed when the object of their eternal affection was absent? When the Singer of the eternal song departed, did heaven go silent?

Heaven rejoiced in the radiance of God's glory for eon upon eon. The love dance transpiring between the Father, the Son, and the Holy Spirit twirled in rhythm from time immortal. The friction from their constant expression of love toward one another created such a warm glow that the universe basked in its light. But then, the Son departed.

How did God feel the day Jesus left heaven to pour Himself into a human body? Visualize the moment that the Trinity's love party stopped. Did God grow lonely for His Son? Did He mourn His loss? Did the Father long for the fellowship they had? Could God suffer the empty nest syndrome?

Yes, God knew the end of the story. He knew His Son would return in victory. But that does not change the loss He must have felt. God the Father sacrificed the immediate presence of Christ to send His Son to earth. Love presents itself in sacrifice.

Jesus intentionally left heaven to become human. Paul describes the heavy price Jesus paid to become one of us:

> Have this mind among yourselves, which is yours in Christ Jesus, who, though he was in the form of God, did not count equality with God a thing to be grasped, but emptied himself, by taking the form of a servant, being born in the likeness of men. Philippians 2:5-7.

What did Jesus willingly give up becoming that Child in

the manger? Christ empties Himself of His divine privileges of all-power, all-knowing, and all-presence to become a vulnerable babe. Beyond that, He also emptied Himself of the heavenly fellowship and glory that He shared with the Father and the Spirit. Before His arrest, Jesus prayed, *I glorified you on earth, having accomplished the work that you gave me to do. And now, Father, glorify me in your own presence with the glory that I had with you before the world existed,* John 17:4–5. I think Jesus also longed for the fellowship of the Father. In my words, Christ was saying, "I want to be with You, Father!"

It is hard for us to fathom the expense the Father, the Son, and the Holy Spirit paid to enable Christ to be born among us. They endured this pain to redeem us from every kindred, tongue, and tribe. God loves us so much that He allowed this great sacrifice to bring you and me into His family. Heaven lost the glory of the Son for a season that we might receive the glory of the Son for eternity.

Heavenly Father, thank you for the price you paid for my salvation. It is hard for me to fathom Your feelings when Your Son left Heaven. The pain you endured watching Your Son suffer on the cross is incalculable. Forgive us, Father, for the pain we have caused You by our sin. I now long to fellowship with You as You and Jesus and the Spirit commune together. Jesus, you lost everything for me, even Your life. I commit my life to serve You, who gave so much to me. Amen.

God Gives Us Music

EARTH RESOUNDS WITH MUSIC

And there were shepherds living out in the fields nearby, keeping watch over their flocks at night. An angel of the Lord appeared to them, and the glory of the Lord shone around them, and they were terrified. But the angel said to them, "Do not be afraid. I bring you good news of great joy that will be for all the people. Today in the town of David a Savior has been born to you; he is Christ the Lord. This will be a sign to you: You will find a baby wrapped in cloths and lying in a manger."

Suddenly a great company of the heavenly host appeared with the angel, praising God and saying,

"Glory to God in the highest, and on earth peace to men on whom his favor rests." Luke 2:8-14

Sheer terror struck the shepherds dumb when they should have been praising. They were afraid when they should have had peace.

Why do we react opposite the way we should when God does something supernatural?

Are we so afraid of things originating in the spiritual realm?

I remember as a young Christian, when people referred to the "Holy Ghost," I always got the jitters conjuring up images of Casper or the Haunted Mansion at Disneyland. God, help me not to be afraid when You want to do something wonderful!

On the other hand, the shepherds are my heroes. They faithfully do their job protecting their sheep from lions, wolves and riff-raff. They sleep in the field because it's necessary for their flock and their families. When I grow up, I want to be as faithful as them.

Can you imagine faithfully working hard at your job when a mighty host of angels suddenly sing in your workplace? Beautiful music, heavenly worship, intoxicating melodies suddenly erupting and drowning out the phones, photocopier, and elevator music. The shepherds were afraid, but I hope I would tap my foot, clap my hands and sing with the angels. What would you do? Too often, fear robs us of our joy!

This is the sign, *a Savior has been born to you; he is Christ the Lord the Savior has been born to you.* A Savior from sin and an Anointed One to deliver us from evil. The shepherds prepare the sheep for eventual sacrifice receive the announcement of the Savior who would be the Lamb of God. The Lamb, Christ, takes away the sin of the world.

Praise is the only right response. The angels gave it; the shepherds joined in and so should we. The Messiah comes to deliver us from our sins, past, present, and future. This is the greatest news in history. God is for us, not against us. He came because He loves us, not so He could smack us down. Stand up and sing with the angels.

I began attending a place where people worshiped by raising their hands to God while they sang. When I tried, I felt so awkward, so conspicuous, as if everybody was looking at me. First Timothy 2:8 says, *I desire therefore that the men pray everywhere, lifting up holy hands, without wrath and doubting* (NKJV).

The Bible says to lift our hands toward God in prayer and worship, so what was holding me back? My focus was on me, and that was the problem. The thought: *what will people think of me?* filled my mind. Instead of focusing on God, I was afraid of what people would think. Fear was robbing me of joy, just like it did the shepherds.

What do angels look like? And what does an angelic host look or sound like? Awesome, I imagine. The incredible nature of this event doesn't translate very well to a Hallmark Christmas Card. God went to great lengths to tell us about His Son and that His favor rests upon us.

What does His favor resting upon us look like?

God's kindness rests on those who believe in His Son. The Greek word translated favor is *eudokia,* meaning God's goodwill has turned toward us bringing peace, prosperity, and rest. We rest in God's unconditional love. He doesn't give up on us.

Yet our mind screams, *so why don't I feel blessed?*

We struggle daily, as life can be so difficult. God requires two things of us for us to live in the joy of His blessing. First, we must choose to trust Him with a steadfast faith through the battle. Second, we need to be thankful for the abundance of His blessing upon our lives. Without thankfulness, we will miss the miracle happening before our eyes, even as the Shepherds did.

Hearts that are thankful see the surrounding beauty. We can hear the angels singing. We are free to respond to God's great blessing upon us because of Jesus. Christ is born, so sing Hallelujah!

Lord God, hear my cry today and open my eyes to Your blessings all around me. Open my ears to hear the beauty of Your song. Remove the fear that makes me hide from you and bow to the desires of others. Sometimes I cower before the supernatural grace You have showered upon me. Help me run through the storm rather than around it. I commit to staying confident in You because I am Yours and You are mine. Today I receive Your Son as my Savior, Deliverer, Grace-Giver, and my Lord, I receive all the blessings they entail. Hope, peace, prosperity, and security are mine in Jesus' name. Thank YOU LORD. *Amen.*

God Gives Us His Name

THE NAME OF JESUS

On the eighth day, when it was time to circumcise him, he was named Jesus, the name the angel had given him before I had conceived him.

When the time of their purification according to the Law of Moses had been completed, Joseph and Mary took him to Jerusalem to present him to the Lord (as it is written in the Law of the Lord, "Every firstborn male is to be consecrated to the Lord"), and to offer a sacrifice in keeping with what is said in the Law of the Lord: "a pair of doves or two young pigeons." Luke 2:21-24

John Lennon mistakenly believed the Beatles were more famous than Christ. While the dead Beatle lies in the grave, Jesus' Name is the most recognized Name in the world.

Two hundred and fifty years ago, the French Enlightenment philosopher Voltaire railed against the authenticity of the Bible. He said Christianity would be extinct within a hundred years. Ironically, within a hundred years of his death, Voltaire is all but forgotten. His home now belongs to the Geneva Bible Society, and that group distributes millions of Bibles from there.

Over two billion people on this planet believe the Bible and trust the Name of Jesus for salvation, hope, and healing. His is the Name that makes demons flee and believers rejoice.

Luke records the endowment of Christ's Name at the Temple in our passage today. The Name of Jesus derives from the Hebrew name Joshua, meaning *The Lord is Salvation.* It is the Name world religions hate because Christians will not bow to Mohammed, Buddha, Krishna or secular humanism.

The Name of Jesus represents the man above all men - God of every God, Light of every Light. It is the Name that sometimes divides families, communities, and nations, dividing between unbelievers and believers. It is the Name above all names, the Name to whom every knee shall bow, and every tongue confesses, *"HE IS LORD."*

There is power in Jesus' Name to break every chain of addiction and unclean habit. The resurrection power exerted by *the Name* robs the grave, strikes the Devil dumb, and sends demons scurrying like lizards on hot rocks. It is the Name by which every sickness must submit, and every affliction must bow.

Jesus demolishes evil kingdoms and causes dictators to tremble. Satan shakes with terror as heaven populates with new believers. Heaven's armies engage the hordes of Hades in battle, reducing that dark dominion to rubble. At the very whisper of the Name of Jesus, Lucifer's power evaporates.

It's been said that Satan no longer recruits on Saturday nights at the local bars, but he goes to church on Sunday mornings. He employs demons of gossip, strife, and condemnation to tempt the faithful. Those fellowships that lift and worship the Name of Jesus cause the devil to flee.

A multitude of biblical metaphors tries to define *the Name*, but it transcends reduction to letters on a page. His Name is Creator God, Mighty Deliverer, and Silent Sacrifice. He is the Captain of our Angel armies, the Dayspring, Desire of the Ages, Lily of the Valley and the Bright and Morning Star. He is the Suffering Messiah and the Conquering Hero. He is our Healer, our Comforter, and our Mighty Baptizer with the Holy Spirit, our Burden Bearer, and our High Priest. *He* became sin for us that we might put on His Righteousness like a royal robe.

Mary and Joseph were simply giving their little boy a name—Jesus—meaning, *God is Salvation.* But one day, when the trumpet of God shall sound, the King with that Name will raise the dead and catch us up in the air to be with Him. He will parade us as trophies of His grace into the very throne room of God. Revelation 19:11-16, *NKJV,* wraps up the holy writ with these words:

Behold, a white horse and He who sat on him was called Faithful and True, and in righteousness He judges and makes war. His eyes were like a flame of fire, and on His head were many crowns. He had a NAME written that no one knew except Himself. He was clothed with a robe dipped in blood, and His name is called The Word of God. And the armies in heaven, clothed in fine linen, white and clean, followed Him on white horses. Now out of His mouth goes a sharp sword, that He should strike the nations. And He Himself will rule them with a rod of iron. He Himself treads the winepress of the fierceness and wrath of Almighty God. And He has on His robe and on His thigh a name written: KING OF KINGS AND LORD OF LORDS. His name is JESUS.

Do you intimately know the power of the Name of Jesus? Does your heart swell with the white-hot heat of His Presence? Do you filter your life decisions through the Name of Jesus? Mary and Joseph showed us how to welcome the newborn King—name Him Jesus!

My Lord, I bow to the power of Your Name. I pray I am known by Your Name and live in the dynamic of Your Name. I ask that I could walk in Your authority this day. Empower me to live for the glory of Your Name. In Jesus' Name I pray. Amen.

Fable 1

THE ORIGINAL CHRISTMAS SONG

Where were you when I laid the earth's foundation?

Tell me, if you understand...

On what were its footings set,

or who laid its cornerstone —

while the morning stars sang together

and all the angels shouted for joy? Job 38:4-7

The Singer sang and time sprang forth. He sang a magnificent song, shaking the worlds into existence. Beautiful music danced through the universe and the sun, moon, and stars waltzed in perfect rhythm. But humanity questioned everything in the song for so long that humans forgot the Singer. That's when the great sadness began. The earth decayed, and the song faded into a distant memory.

God fashioned the heavens and the earth while the stars sang. We look through the eyes of science and we see laser beams and light-years calculated to infinity. But we miss the song and the Singer. God speaks the language of beauty and design while science seeks the method and math of creation. Albert Einstein said, "Science is lame without religion and religion without science is blind." Science relates to creation as sheet music interacts with a song. Both are necessary, but methodology must follow the creative genius.

Creation resounds in the glory of God. But humanity has a problem called sin. It mucks up the works considerably. The hurts and pains deafened people to the song. It blinded them from seeing the splendor. The fatal flaw can be traced back to the Garden of Eden, where Adam and Eve rebelled against God. Humankind inherited their mutinous nature and passed it on from generation to generation. They were not trying to be bad—it just came naturally. All seemed hopeless until the Father of music created a new beginning.

God's secret plan slowly unfolded. In the stillness of a Middle Eastern night, a Hebrew named Abraham once again heard the stars sing. The promise revealed to Abraham that salvation would come through his descendants. And he believed the promise. God would create a new song for humanity to sing and rejoin the praises of the morning stars.

The Holy Child was born in Bethlehem, birthed to the tune of "Glory to God in the highest." The universe sang at His birth, "At once the angel was joined by a huge angelic choir singing God's praises: Glory to God in the heavenly heights, Peace to all men and women on earth who please him." Luke 2:13-14 (THE MESSAGE)

Humanity crucified Jesus the Savior, but God's creative song is unquenchable. All creation groaned until the dissonance of pain and suffering converted to the melody of resurrection. The great sadness morphed into joy. This message of life unshackles people who have faith in Christ.

The song of creation and Christmas simmers in every Christian's spirit. They are God's psalmists. His creative song dances in many hearts, waiting to be sung. The universe is longing to hear the new thing that God has created in you.

Christmas is the melody of the ages, and we sing in harmony with the Singer. The angels sang it and invited the shepherds and all people to embrace their joy. The birth of Jesus is our theme: "It came upon a midnight clear, that glorious song of old, From angels bending near the earth, To touch their harps of gold: Peace on the earth, goodwill to men, From heaven's all-gracious King."

Christmas Jesus

Fable 2

WHEN GOD CALLED SAINT NICK

We couldn't sleep on Christmas Eve, so we snickered and played the guessing game. We taunted one another with our imagined gifts to open on Christmas morning. "Guess what I'm getting for Christmas," we snickered, and made so much noise that Mom eventually came up to our room. We pretended to be asleep, but she called our bluff.

"I know you're awake, so quit trying to fool me. I have a Christmas Eve story to tell, so lie still and listen."

Gabriel, the Arch Angel, announced before heaven's throne, "Your Majesty, the children are restless."

"What? My children?" mused the Ancient Glorious Wonder.

The nine-foot angel whined, "The children of the realm stir impatiently waiting for something more."

"Why, I gave them everything they could need. Mothers to nurture and fathers to challenge them and grandparents to lavish My love upon them. What more could they want?"

"Perhaps the dark stain still shadows their hearts, Father," said the Son as He entered the eternal throne room. "Greed and selfishness lurk in their imaginations."

"Aye, it shades their minds from comprehending the gift of My great love for them." The foundations of heaven shook as the Father stood to make a pronouncement. Raising the scepter of His power, He thundered the pronouncement, "I propose gifts for all the children of the realm, gifts to delight and gifts to make merry the hearts of children everywhere. Call Saint Nick to create a plan to carry out my decree." With the thunderclap of His scepter upon the sea of glass before His throne, the decree went forth.

Millions of heavenly creatures flapped their wings and bowed their heads before the wondrous wisdom of the Ancient Father. But *how* could Saint Nick possibly carry out the royal decree?

Paradise resumed its singing, and Cherubim blew the horns of holiness day and night. Soon, the halls of heaven rattled with the joy-filled cry of Saint Nick, "Ho, Ho, Ho! Gather round seraphim and angels galore, for I have a plan to carry the Father's love to the ends of the earth. An abundance of life evermore for all who believe and receive fullness of life. Father will write peace and joy in the sky and etch it in human hearts. We need food in abundance, beautiful wrappings, and lights to brighten the celebrations."

The Holy One's laughter reverberated through all creation, "I knew Saint Nick would invent a plan to fill my children's hearts with joy."

Saint Nick bowed before the Ancient of Days, "Yes, Great Father, but there is a price."

He decreed with nostrils flaring and hair flying, interrupting Saint Nick, "No price is too much for *My* children, no extravagance too generous for My love."

"But what is the price?" the angels cried.

Saint Nick's shoulders shook, and he heaved with sobs of travail. "Father, Your children long for fame and money. They desire to be given whatever they can imagine. The dark stain holds them as slaves and blinds them to the gift of Your love. They fight and argue while lusting for more, evermore."

Not a wing fluttered. Breathless angels hung still as heaven waxed silent. Finally, the angels whispered, "So what is the price?"

All heaven wept, "Who is worthy to pay the price? Who can heal the blindness that blocks the vision of God's love?"

"The children need to see, the children need to see, the children need to see," chanted the seraphim.

Just then, the object of the Father's love for eon upon eon stepped up to heaven's heights. His hair was white like wool and His face shining like the sun, His garments shone like burnished brass and His voice like the sound of many waters— the Son, the Apple of the Father's eye, said, "I will pay the price, I will go to Bethlehem to be the baby born to die. Then the children will see the ultimate gift and they will want no more."

Slowly, the Son dropped the robe of His power and shed the scepter of His authority. He laid down His glory and left heaven silent.

Whispers and whirring of angel armies set all heaven abuzz with the cry, "What could this mean?"

The Father rose from His throne. "Gabriel, it's time. Blow the trumpet. Angels form into choirs. Guardians of light burn a pathway to the City of David—a baby is born this night to fulfill my promises."

Launching into action, all heaven jumped at the Father's commands. Then sleigh bells and reindeer hoofs split the skies.

"Ho, Ho, Ho, Merry Christmas!" shouted Saint Nick with glee. "The light of the world has come. The Son of the Most-High God is born in a manger. The Gift of all gifts blesses all children everywhere. May the Son heal blind eyes and cleanse the dark stain with His own blood. Children everywhere rejoice, the Lamb of God who takes away the sins of the world has come!"

Suddenly a great company of the heavenly host appeared with the angel, praising God and saying, "Glory to God in the highest, and on earth peace to men on whom his favor rests."

Mom finished her story and said, "Sleep now little children. Dream as I dream. I dream of the Son given to you, the Son who can drive dark stains from hearts. Sleep now. Dream of what you can give on Christmas morning, for it is in the giving that genuine joy will flood your heart. Giving what matters most is the price of Christmas. God gave us the life of

His Son with all His love. Now we must give to one another with all our love."

Fable 3

BECOMING

The hope of the righteous will be gladness, but the expectation of the wicked will perish. Proverbs 10:28

Miss Judith was an older schoolteacher in the 1930s, back in the day when people believed a woman's place was at home with the family. In her youth, she had a few suitors vie for her affections, but she never really felt loved. So, she didn't marry.

The fifth-grade grammar school students thought of her as an old maid. They whispered cruel jokes when they thought she couldn't hear them. But she never let on that their words hurt her feelings. Miss Judith enjoyed her students, and she loved them regardless.

Holidays with her sister's family were a highlight of Miss Judith's life. Gift wrapping galore, delicious food followed by scrumptious desserts, and children running about trying out their new toys was the order of the day. It was such a hoot watching her nieces and nephews open their gifts.

The boys would eventually terrorize the neighborhood with wooden toy guns while the girls dressed their dolls. Her sister always helped Judith to feel a part of the family festivities.

At the end of the day, she would board the train that carried her home to her little, quiet apartment in the city.

This Christmas had the usual celebrations, fun yet so exhausting. She was glad to be home to a peaceful house, even if it was a bit dreary. Some would call her lonely and boring. She thought life had simply passed her by and would live out her days in quiet resignation.

The city looked dreary that day through the train window. A light drizzle was falling on the dirty black pavement. Though it was only late afternoon, the streetlights were already coming on. Plugging along, she made her way home, up the drab concrete stairway to her apartment. She preferred the stairs to the elevator because it often was the only exercise she got.

Judith's place sat with well-appointed furniture and lacey curtains. The apartment was odd because it had no masculine mess, no newspapers lying about, no tools in the closets or sports equipment in the corners. Tidy was teacher Judith's residence. The muted hush of a childless home hangs heavy.

Laying her gifts on the dining room table gave her a moment of disdainful pleasure. More gloves to add to her collection and another set of furry slippers to keep an old maid's feet warm. As the day wore into dusk, she felt a nap creeping into her soul. Drearily, she made her way to the couch and, with one last look out the window to the graying city below, she lay down. The Christmas sugar treats had long spent their energy, and her body was calling for a lazy snooze. She hoped to avoid the lonely discontent that was her nightly attendant.

Slowly drifting into a dream, Judith found herself in a bright garden-like meadow. The place sparkled with light and a brilliant blue sky, yet there was no sun in the sky.

She walked beside a gently flowing stream among the low growing grasses. There was a peace unlike she had ever known. The noise of nature–water, birds and the rustling of a wind full of butterflies flitting from flower to flower–were the music in that place.

"Where am I, what strange place is this?" She pondered.

In the distance, she saw two women approaching slowly on the other side of the stream. One was tall and lithe, more beautiful in her primitive vitality than any women Judith had ever seen. Over six feet tall, with muscular arms and legs pulsating with vigor, she exuded energy. A flowing white cotton dress sheathed the Amazon-like woman.

Beside her, another woman limped and swayed as she walked. She was not unlovely, but a pervasive sadness overshadowed her entire being. Somehow, she resembled the taller woman as if they were sisters. Though slower and more deliberate, she headed in the same direction as the taller woman.

The companions saw Miss Judith and beckoned her to travel with them, they on their side of the stream and she on hers. They never spoke, but their hand motions conveyed their message–they wanted her to follow. Judith didn't know where they were going on this mystical journey, but she would enjoy the adventure.

Amazon Woman, as Judith came to think of her, was so intent on her journey. She strode with more and more determination. Her companion soon fell behind. Judith felt sorry for her and wanted to say to their leader, *Slow down, let the poor woman catch up.* But the leader's pace only quickened in intensity with every passing mile. Driven like a woman possessed by hidden purpose, she sped up her pace to a light run. Judy envied her ability, her fitness, the resolve that drove her.

The schoolteacher ran to keep up and occasionally glanced back to see the poor companion fading into the distance. The weaker woman was not giving up. She continued to limp along.

Amazon Woman gained speed, making every stride stretch. Her arms stroked the wind, plunging forward in an earthy rhythm melding wind, sky and earth. Judith marveled, *"Where did such a creature come from?"*

The middle-aged schoolteacher was clearly not accustomed to such rigorous exercise. Something about the air in this place enabled her to continue to run, struggle though she must, to keep up with this driven woman.

Faster and faster they ran, each on their own side of the stream. Limpy, far in the distance, was barely visible. Finally, Amazon slowed down, resting beside the stream. Knelling warrior style beside the water, she cupped her hands to scoop sips into her mouth. Her eyes scanned the distance upstream.

As Judith followed her gaze, she saw a distant man approaching. Captivated by the unfamiliar figure, Judith panted to catch her breath and gulped some water.

The stranger was older than Judith, but as fit as the Amazon woman. This scarred and rugged figure **approached them.** Amazon's demeanor completely changed in the man's presence. Her constant motion settled. Serenity enveloped her consciousness. Her countenance conveyed energy and vitality, yet she sat strangely still, waiting.

Was he coming to meet us? Would he halt our journey with some cosmic message? Could he bring conversation to this silent place? When he came near, he nodded to Amazon as if to commend her and say, *Well done in the journey.* Judith knew intuitively that he was the destination of their journey. Amazon's untamed beauty, her athletic prowess and her driven nature rested peacefully in his presence.

The man looked up at Judith, the teacher—he on one side of the stream and she on the other. His mouth moved as if to call out to her. She heard only a whisper, so she waded into the stream to draw closer to him. His chest heaved as he seemed to bellow out, and Judith grasped his voice faintly. *"Come closer,"* he cried as he waded into the stream. She stepped deeper into the water to approach the sound of his voice.

Can you hear me, child? The rugged one said.

She had so much she wanted to ask him, but she didn't know what to say. She eked out, "Yes, I hear you. Where are we, sir?"

He thought for a moment and answered, "we are where the ordinary becomes glorious and the glorious is ordinary. Was the journey difficult?"

"Yes, but that beautiful woman led the way, and she was relentless in pursuing her destination. She is so strong and limber, like no woman I have ever seen. Can you tell me, Sir, who is she?"

"Why daughter of Eve, don't you know?"

"She is you and all that you shall become. She is all the Father created you to be." His words stunned Judith.

"But, but, then who is the other woman coming behind us?" Judith asked?

The rugged one responded, "She is all that you have been. She is the cocoon you are leaving behind."

Miss Judith pondered his words and asked, "then what is the meaning of my life?"

"The importance of your life lies in what you are becoming. You fill your life with meaning when you give it in pursuit of a higher purpose. Many are growing older, but not wiser. Some are decaying in body but without growing vital in their spirit. Self-centered and isolated, their heart yearns to be given away in loving purpose."

Then Judith awoke from her Christmas dream. Not a stick of furniture moved, but everything had changed. She still had no husband, no children to call her own. No house in the suburbs, no family filling her home. But now her future brimmed with potential. Becoming what the Father created her to be filled her heart with desire.

Judith realized her purpose was being worked out on earth, while her faith anchored her in another land. Her destination, now revealed, is another place and her road beckons with fresh inspiration.

Judith is a daughter of Eve, becoming all God created her to be thanks to a gift wrapped in a Christmas nap.

*The greatest thing in the world is
not so much where we are, but in what
direction we are moving.*

Oliver Wendell Holmes

About the Author

Dave Holland lives to help people become more like Jesus. It is his mission to *Love God and Love People.* He has walked with God for over 50 years. He pastored churches for 37 years but has also learned that the church and Jesus are not the same. Jesus is the only true center.

Dave planted a thriving church in Brockton, Massachusetts starting with just sixteen people and from that church, he mothered seven other congregations in Massachusetts. He also pastored a church in Uxbridge, Massachusetts that grew to near a thousand people in its constituency.

Dave attended Life Pacific College, graduating in 1979 and ordained by the Foursquare Movement in 1981. While pastoring in New England, he received his Master of Arts Degree from Gordon-Conwell Theological Seminary graduating Magnum Cum Laude in 1997. He says of his seminary experience, "God spoke to me the first day I attended classes that 'education tends to pride—study hard but don't let it go to your head.'" He recently graduated with a Master of Arts degree in English from Grand Canyon University in 2019.

Reach out to him at davidvholland54@gmail.com.

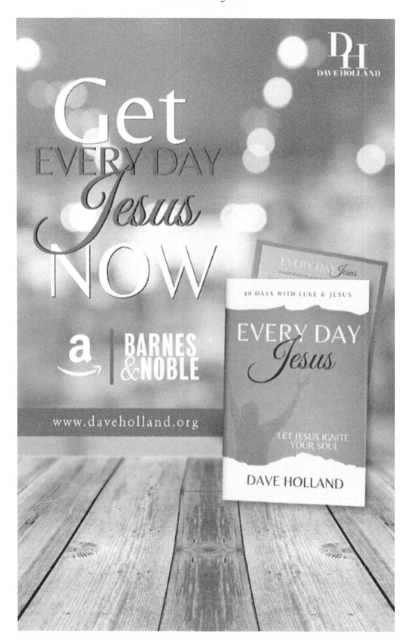

Made in the USA
Monee, IL
06 May 2022

96008640R00030